THE
Archive Photographs
SERIES

NEWPORT
WEST OF THE RIVER

Best wishes

Alex Dawson.

Coal trimmers, Alexandra Docks, c. 1910. The coal trimmer's job was to distribute the coal load in the ship's hold correctly. Their work was vitally important for the safety of the ship as well as highly labour intensive. The trimmers are holding the special shovels used for the job.

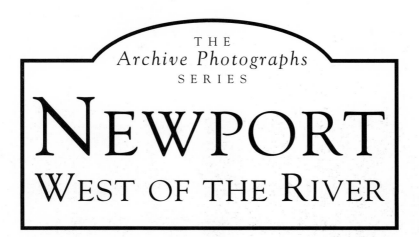

THE
Archive Photographs
SERIES

NEWPORT
WEST OF THE RIVER

Compiled by
Alex Dawson
from the collections of
Newport Museum and Art Gallery

CHALFORD

First published 1995
Copyright © Newport Museum and Art Gallery, 1995

The Chalford Publishing Company
St Mary's Mill, Chalford,
Stroud, Gloucestershire, GL6 8NX

ISBN 0 7524 0338 9

Typesetting and origination by
The Chalford Publishing Company
Printed in Great Britain by
Redwood Books, Trowbridge

Aerial view of Newport, April 1928. Landmarks to look for are: the Lyceum in Bridge Street (now demolished), St Paul's Church on Commercial Street, St Mary's Roman Catholic Church on Stow Hill and Dock Street running parallel with the railway to the docks. This photograph was taken before the Civic Centre was built in Clytha Park.

Contents

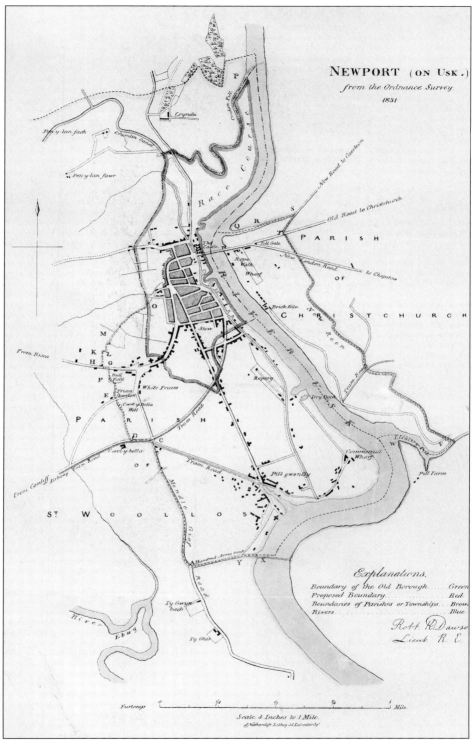

Map showing Newport in 1831 produced by the Ordnance Survey.

Children from the Scannell family photographed at Busby's Studio, Church ~~Street~~, 1904.
ROAD

Introduction

Newport Museum and Art Gallery was opened on 21 May 1888 by the Mayor of the town, Thomas Pugsley. At the time the Museum Committee 'earnestly solicited suitable donations of Art and Natural History specimens, and other objects, from gentlemen in the town' and were richly rewarded. The people of Newport have been adding to the museum collections ever since and photographs have proved to be a significant and important part of their donations.

This book holds a selection of about 200 photographs of Newport west of the river, taken from the thousands in the Museum and Art Gallery archives. The strength of our photographic archive lies in the fact that it is so wide-ranging, recording every day lives as well as once in a lifetime occasions. The photographs selected for this book are a constant reminder that life is both ever changing and ever the same: although the camera shows us familiar scenes, personal memories of family life, work, schooldays and holidays, we are at the same time seeing life as it was lived in another age. The people of Newport can be justly proud of this unique record of their lives and achievements. We are constantly acquiring new photographs and I am looking forward to working on a second volume illustrating life on the east side of the Usk.

This collection echoes the energy and enthusiasm of the nineteenth century, an era when Newport was justifiably proud of its manufacturing industries, its trading links with the world, and its sons and daughters. We are reminded of the spirit of another age when the face of Newport and its attendant industries was very different.

While researching for this book I came across an after dinner toast given at the beginning of this century in Newport. It is, I think, a fitting tribute to the history and heritage of Newport:

I give you a Toast!

NEWPORT
For
IMPORT, TRANSPORT, EXPORT -
MY PORT, YOUR PORT,
OUR PORT!

Alex Dawson
Keeper of Human History, Newport Museum and Art Gallery

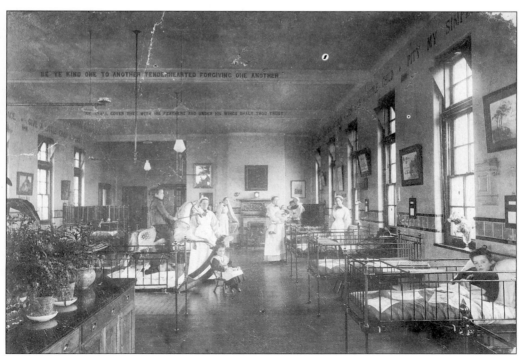

Tredegar Children's Ward, Royal Gwent Hospital, about 1910. The ward was opened in 1901 and demolished in 1992.

One
Docks and River

Newport pilot cutter, the *Charlotte Annie*, probably c. 1890. Pilot cutters travelled the coast from Bristol and Newport across to Ireland, and down as far as Land's End, looking for ships to guide into harbour. The small sailing boats were renowned for their speed, just as the pilots themselves were famous for their sailing skill and knowledge of the coastline. The *Charlotte Annie* was built by Mordey, Carney & Co. in 1878. It was owned by Samuel John Small, who was a Newport pilot for 40 years.

The *Welsh Prince* steam boat, moored below Town Bridge, before 1886. The boat belonged to T. Mitchell, owner of the Bristol and Newport Screw Steam Packet Company. Daily services ran between Newport and Bristol carrying passengers, livestock and merchandise. The service was discontinued in 1886 due to competition from the newly opened Severn Tunnel.

Crawshay Bailey opening the Alice Dry Dock, owned by Mordey, Carney & Co., 1871.

Town Dock, from the roof of the Orb Steel Works on the east side of the river, after 1895. This was the earliest dock in Newport, built in 1842 at a cost of £200,000.

Workmen, possibly at the Commercial Dry Dock inside the Alexandra North Dock, c. 1900. The ship is in for repairs.

Gathering coal for domestic use on the Severn Estuary at the mouth of the River Ebbw, c. 1900.

Advertisement for the Westgate Hotel, 1903. The Westgate was the major hotel in Newport. This advertisement emphasises the Westgate's important links with the business and industrial communities.

The Westgate Hotel

The Principal Hotel in Newport.

Telephone 410.

Re-furnished, Re-decorated, and Modernized.   Finest Cuisine and Wines.

Quite Up-to-date in
every way.

Electric Light.

Night Porter.

Moderate Charges.

Large Stock Rooms.

First-class
Accommodation for
Meetings, &c.

Three Minutes from
Station.

Within easy distance
of Docks.

Send for descriptive Tariff, Post Free on application to E. H. WATTS.

NEWPORT, Mon.

Below: The *Maria Margretta Timra*, a Swedish ship, unloading timber in the Alexandra North Dock, c. 1905. Timber for use as pit props was one of the main imports into Newport. In front of the ship a man can be seen fastening the timber into rafts so that it can be floated out of the dock for storage.

Installation of coal hoists, probably at Alexandra South Dock, 1907. Coal hoists at this dock were capable of shipping coal at the rate of 800 tons per hour each.

A steam concrete mixer in use during the construction of Alexandra South Dock, 1908.

Building the sea lock to the Alexandra Dock South Dock extension which was opened in 1914. The chambers behind the workmen are repeated on the opposite side of the lock. The small lower chambers allowed the water to be pumped in and out, while the larger chamber above held the main gate.

Town Dock, c. 1890. The building to the left is a warehouse.

Outside the Seaman's Union at 31 Ruperra Street, c. 1910.

Children taking food to their fathers who were working on Alexandra North Dock, after 1906. The ship is Swedish, and is unloading timber. The Transporter Bridge can be seen in the background.

Tugs leaving the sea lock to the Alexandra Docks south extension to bring a vessel in, after 1914. The "Holman" tugboat to the right belonged to the Newport Screw Towing Co. Ltd and was built in 1908.

Two
Trade and Industry

The Old Customs House in Skinner Street, c. 1900. The Customs House was next door to the home of the Customs Collector, Marmaduke Brewer. It held offices for two clerks, the Receiver of Lights and Merchant Seamen's Dues, the Collector, the Comptroller, Tide Surveyors, tidewaiters and boatmen. In addition, the Collector's daughters used the house to give dancing lessons, for which Fiddler Jacobs provided the music. In 1856 the Customs House moved to Dock Street after it had outgrown this accommodation in Skinner Street. The furniture warehouse to the right of the Customs House is an estate agent's today.

Architectural drawing of the Corn Exchange by the architect, Benjamin Lawrence, 1870s. The Corn Exchange was built in 1878 in memory of Lord Tredegar's services to agriculture and farming. It was paid for by public subscription and built on land leased from Lord Tredegar at a peppercorn rent. Corn dealers bought and sold corn there and paid a rent which covered the upkeep of the building. It ceased to be used as an exchange in 1935 and was eventually demolished around 1980 as part of the ring road development.

The Devon and Cornwall House, at 9
Dock Parade, c. 1890. The proprietor of
this beer house was Timothy Leary and
may be the gentleman standing to the
left.

A laundry, possibly in Pill, c. 1900.

The original staff of Lovell and Co. Ltd in their premises in Albany Street, 1897. Lovells became so famous for their Toffee Rex, advertised as the 'King of Toffees', that their factory built at Crindau in 1893 became known as 'Rexville.' Mr George Frederick Lovell, the founder of the business is seated in the front row, arms folded, looking to his right. William Smith, aged 14, is seated to the right in the same row, arms folded and wearing a hat. William became a master confectioner, specialising in making lettered rock and Russian toffee.

Lovell's delivery van, c. 1910. Lovell's confectionary was distributed in their own fleet of vans which were maintained in their own workshops. Giles & Williams were a local coach building firm in Shaftesbury Street.

Finishing a large industrial basket at William Garlands, basketmakers, 101 Commercial Street, c. 1905.

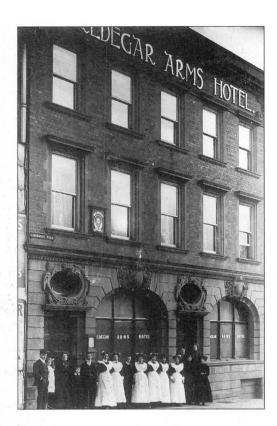

The entire staff of the Tredegar Arms Hotel, Cambrian Road, 1906.

The lounge of the Tredegar Arms Hotel, 1906.

Uskside Smithy, Uskside Engineering and Rivet Co. Ltd, 1912. The business was started in 1827 in Church Street by William Evans and manufactured anchors and chains. At the time this photograph was taken the business had moved to the riverside, near the Tredegar Dry Dock. By this time the managing director, Arthur Stevens, was turning his interests to the coal mining industry and the range of products had been extended to cover specialised colliery winding gear and haulage equipment.

W.A. Baker's Westgate Foundry, c. 1900. Dock Street is to the left of the photographer with Skinner Street to the right. Baker's were a major employer in the town at this time and described themselves as bridge builders and structural engineers. This building was probably Baker's original foundry, although by the time this photograph was taken it was described as a warehouse and showrooms.

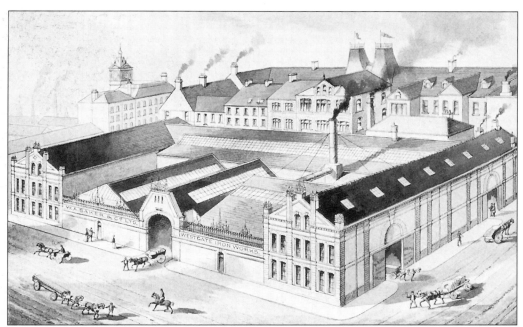

Pictorial view of the Westgate Foundry from W.A. Baker's catalogue for 1905. The Town Hall on Commercial Street can be seen to the back left. The two small towers back right stood above Baker's Commercial Street showroom, and can still be seen today above Burton Menswear.

W.A. Baker's Central Ironworks, from Baker's catalogue for 1905. Caroline Street is to the left of the picture, running at right angles to Dock Parade. A huge variety of cast and wrought iron ware was made here, including the cast iron supports for the Dock Street museum (see page 66) and the balustrade for Charles Street Baptist Church (see page 78).

Staff outside Baker's Central Ironworks, c. 1900.

The castle photographed from the river before 1899. During the nineteenth century the castle was converted to a variety of uses including a tannery, warehouse, nail factory and lastly a brewery. It was renovated by the Ministry of Works in 1930.

Staff of Vile Bros., aerated water manufacturers, at the Phoenix Soda Water Works, in Alma Street, after 1910.

Vile Bros. delivery van, c. 1920.

Advertisement for Vile Bros., 1905.

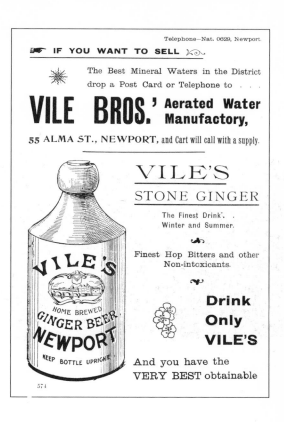

Coal merchant's cart built for G.W. Parry by Allen Bros. of Newport. The coal wagons in the background have brought coal to Newport from the Cannop coalfields in the Forest of Dean.

Breaking up the *Doric*, a Cunard White Star liner, at Cashmores, 1935. John Cashmore Ltd was founded in 1912 and was renowned for works dismantling and shipbreaking.

Dismantling the old Town Bridge in 1926-27. The stone arches of the old bridge were removed by placing arched supports underneath them. It was said that the bridge was demolished without dropping a single stone into the river. The temporary bridge which served while the new crossing was under construction can be seen in the background.

Cutting corn at Bassaleg, 1930s. The field is Gorse Field which was farmed by Horace Stephens. Pen-y-lan Close and Caerphilly Road have replaced these fields today. Harry Hicks is leading the horses, two of which were called Fashion and Bowler.

Haymaking at Bassaleg, 1931. Harry Hicks is holding the pitchfork, and Leslie Bond, Gilbert Tanner, Clement Hargest and Cyril Bond are on the hayrick. Mr Powell of Tub Row is standing to the right of the children. The Parish Church of St Basils can be seen in the background.

F. Prosser & Son loading sheep at the Cattle Market in the 1930s..

Prosser & Son's lorry decorated for the Coronation, Lyne Road, 1937

Painting Town Bridge in readiness for the visit of King George VI, 1937.

Inspecting a new acquisition for the museum, December 1938. To the right is Mr Goffe, museum caretaker and to the left, Miss Jose Foster, museum assistant. The bicycle was donated by Thomas Henry Vile of Vile Bros., aerated water manufacturers.

The Museum and Art Gallery, 7 September 1935. The curator, William Alexander Gunn is sorting exhibits with Miss M. Meek, museum assistant.

Robert Wynn & Sons moving a tank under the railway bridge, Shaftesbury Street, 1950s. Wynn's, of Albany Street, was established in Newport in 1863. The company specialised in moving heavy loads and employed 87 people in Newport by the time the company ceased to exist in 1981.

Wynn's moving a girder at Old Green Crossing, 1960s. The girder was made by Braithwaites and Co. an engineering firm still at Neptune Works on Mill Parade, but now known as Rowecord Engineering Ltd.

Three
Streets and Buildings

The Bridge Hotel, looking towards High Street from Town Bridge, before 1892. The proprietor of the hotel was F.M. Sylvester. The Corn Exchange can be seen on the right hand side of High Street.

Bridge Hotel Stables from Town Bridge, before 1892. The Bridge Hotel was demolished in 1892, and was replaced by the Shaftesbury Temperance Café.

Town Bridge from High Street, before 1892. The Bradbury & Co. sewing machine depot can just be seen on the right. On the opposite side of the road is an ironmongers shop owned by E.S. Eveleigh.

High Street, before 1890. On the left is the Post Office and Corn Exchange, to the right is
Fennell's, fishmonger and poulterer. The pillared porch of the King's Head can be seen just
beyond Fennell's. A horse omnibus is moving towards Town Bridge.

X NOT SHOWN

TRAM

? 1894

Ridgeway from the Monmouthshire Canal, 1895.

The entrance to Shaftesbury Street from High Street, c. 1894. The Castle Hotel rises above the railway line linking Dock Street Station with Mill Street Station. The buildings in front of the Castle, including Eveleigh's ironmongery (see page 40) were demolished shortly before this photograph was taken.

Brynglas Hill from Barrack Hill, c. 1900. Houses under construction are visible along Malpas Road. The newly completed All Saints Church is to the left of an undeveloped Brynglas Road.

All Saints Church and vicarage, Brynglas Road, c. 1900. All Saints was demolished in 1994.

Thatched cottage in the Gold Tops area, c. 1900.

Taxis waiting in Station Approach, 1923. The photographer is standing in front of the railway station, Cambrian Road is to the right. Soon after this was taken the approach was widened, losing the Rialto Cinema on the corner of High Street (see page 107).

A scene from your city long ago

GRASSROOTS 14.7.05

DAYS GONE BY: The picture on the left shows a Newport scene in 1923. The vehicles in the foreground are taxis waiting in Station Approach. The photographer is standing in front of the railway station, with Cambrian Road on the right. Soon after this was taken the approach was widened, so losing the Rialto cinema on the corner of High Street.

Picture taken from Newport West of the River, compiled by Alex Dawson, from the collections of Newport Museum and Art Gallery, published by the Chalford Publishing Company, St Mary's Mill, Chalford, Stroud, Gloucestershire.

Michael and Karen say 'I do'

THE wedding took place at St Paul's Church, Newbridge, of Karen Julie Smith, daughter of Paul and Maureen Smith, of Newbridge, and Michael John Badham, son of Jack and Marie Badham, also of Newbridge.

The bridesmaids were, matron of honour Leah Kinsey (bride's sister), Nicola Goodwin (bride's best friend); pageboys Jordan and Liam Smith (bride's sons), Lee Smith (bride's brother).

The best men were Paul Badham and Mark Goodwin.

The ushers were Curtis Badham (groom's son), Dean Smith (bride's brother), Jonathan Watkins (couple's friend).

The reception was held at the Manor Hotel, Crickhowell.

King's Head Hotel, before 1900. The King's Head was built in 1797. In 1900 it was partially destroyed by fire and the building we know today took its place.

Brynglas Road and All Saints Church, 1927

Housing development, Brynglas Road, 10 January 1927.

46

Bassaleg Toll House shortly before demolition in the 1930s.

St Mary's Lodge, Fields Road, shortly before demolition to make way for the new Civic Centre, 1930s. The lodge was part of the Clytha Park Estate, owned by Miss Watson, daughter of Sir Thomas Watson. The new Civic Centre was opened in 1939. The architect was T. Cecil Howitt.

Bettws Lane, 1959.

High Street on a Saturday afternoon outside Pleasance & Harper, January 1959.

Looking towards the estuary from the tower of St Woolos, May 1959. Landmarks to look out for are: the Royal Gwent Hospital, Belle Vue Secondary School (now demolished), the Alexandra Docks, the gasometer, and Uskmouth Power Station (soon to be demolished).

The Corn Exchange, High Street, during demolition, June 1971.

50

Four
Transport

A horse omnibus entering High Street from Bridge Street about 1893. The roof of the Lyceum can just be seen at the top of the photograph. The first horse omnibus service in Newport was started by George Masters in 1845. The bus ran from George Master's Wine and Spirit Vaults at 2 Bridge Street to the Devonshire House Inn at Church Street, Pillgwenlly, and the fare was 4d. The journey took half an hour. There were no official stopping places for horse buses, they were hailed in the same way that we would stop a London taxi today.

Horse omnibus belonging to the Newport Tramways Company, 1886. This bus was bought from Mr Solomon Andrews, a coach builder in Cardiff. No tickets were issued on the buses, passengers dropped their fares into a box and the conductor filled in a way-bill. If the way-bill and the money box did not tally at the end of the day the conductor had to pay the difference even though passengers often dropped in penny-sized washers. Numbered tickets were introduced in 1901.

Newport Tramways Company staff, 1880s. Drivers and conductors on the trams worked from 8.00 a.m. to 10.00 p.m. with an hour break. Horse tram drivers wore bowler hats in winter and boaters in summer.

Level crossing over the main line of the Great Western Railway at the end of Thomas Street, 1870s. On the right is the Royal Oak Inn, birthplace of John Frost and directly in front of the photographer is the King's Head.

Entrance to Marshes Road underneath the main line of the Great Western Railway, before improvement in 1876. Marshes Road connected with the top of High Street and became Shaftesbury Street in 1905. Most of this area has now been replaced by the Old Green Interchange.

Great Western Railway (Pill Bank branch) level crossing at the end of Commercial Road, before 1900.

Laying tramlines above St Woolos
Church, early 1900s. A horse bus
service ran up Stow Hill to the
Handpost between 1895 and 1902
but it was unprofitable partly
because two horses were needed to
move the buses up the steep
gradient. Stow Hill had no public
transport until the electric tramway
opened in 1904.

The first tram up Stow Hill, June
1904.

Soldiers guarding Station Approach in Newport during the Railway Strike, 19 August 1911.

A No. 18 tram approaching Town Bridge from High Street, c. 1905. The Shaftesbury Café can be seen on the left.

Stage Coach waiting at the King's Head Hotel, c. 1912.

First female tram conductor, 1914.
Women were first employed on Newport
public transport during the First World
War to replace men who had joined the
armed services.

Electric tram at Dock Gates, 1921. The driver (right) is Trevor Watkins and the conductor is Reginald Dando.

Motorbus, 1924. This was the second motorbus to be bought by Newport Corporation Transport and cost £5,081. The service between Bridge Street and Edward VII Avenue began on 12 April 1924.

The Monmouthshire and Brecon Canal looking towards Old Green Crossing probably in the 1930s. The Shaftesbury Café can be seen to the right of the canal. The timber to the right belongs to Nicholas and Co., timber merchants in Screw Packet Road.

The construction of the Kingsway by-pass, early 1930s. The line of the canal lies beneath the road and the Shaftesbury Café can be seen disappearing in front of the road. The by-pass was opened in November 1934.

New ticket machines issued to Newport Corporation Transport staff in the 1950s.

A Fowler traction engine at the parade to celebrate the centenary of heavy hauliers, Robert Wynn and Sons, 1963.

Kingsway photographed from the Market Hall, c. 1950. Newport Corporation Bus Station is in the foreground.

The main line of the Monmouthshire Canal rising through Fourteen Locks outside Newport, probably in the 1950s.

The M4 approaching the Brynglas tunnels during construction, 1965.

Five
Education

National Schools, Commercial Street around 1900. In 1811 'The National Society for Promoting the Education of the Poor in the Principles of the Established Church' was founded, and as a result National Schools were purpose-built all over the country. The society promoted the monitorial method of teaching to show that large numbers of poor children could be educated at a low cost, the system being based on children teaching each other. The Newport National Schools for Boys, Girls and Infants stood opposite St Paul's Church; they were built in 1839 and demolished in 1914. In 1848 the schools were described as 'capacious, lofty and airy'.

A National School class in 1890. The class teacher, or 'assistant' is Elizabeth Robinson, aged about 18. Elizabeth was the grandmother of the bride pictured on page 78.

Certificate of Merit awarded to Elizabeth Robinson while she was a pupil at the National School, 1881.

The National Schools' Mistress (centre), Miss H. Williams, and her assistants, in 1890. Elizabeth Robinson stands at the back, right hand side.

A school visit to the Museum and Art Gallery, Dock Street, in 1912.

The British School, Stow Hill, was built in 1846 on the site later occupied by Queen's High School. British Schools were run on similar lines to the National Schools, although they were non-denominational. The first schoolmaster was the Revd M. Bright, an Independent minister.

Rogerstone Infants class, Group 3, c. 1905.

Boy Scouts, 1st Rogerstone Scout Troop, 1910. On the left is Thomas George Jenkins and on the right is Martin Redvers Jenkins.

Alexandra Road Girls Elementary School, Pillgwenlly, 1900.

The 'Ragged School', Dock Street, 1870s. 'Ragged Schools' were privately run and often children could come and go as they pleased. The Ragged School was also used as a free library in 1881 while the new library was being built in Dock Street. Today this building is a needle exchange.

Bolt Street Elementary School, Pillgwenlly, 1918. The decorations are possibly to celebrate the end of the First World War.

Alexandra Road Elementary School, Pillgwenlly, 1923.

Standard V, St Woolos Elementary School, 2 March 1943. From left to right, back row: Pamela Harris, Joan Anstice, Shirley Macey, Jill Haberfield, Margaret Williams, Joyce Ready, Dorothy Cox, Caroline Jones, Jill Scannell, Barbara Chandler. Third row: Margery Tutt, Mary Hale, Bronwen Jones, Margaret Johnson, Cynthia Smith, Ruth Frich, Joyce Allan, Yvonne Worton, Mary Jones, Sheila James. Second row: Mary Hunt, Anne Lewis, Audrey Camden, Veronica Crabbe, Sheila Hunt, Myra Bevis, Mary Knapman, Joyce Vaughan, Angela Cookson. Front row: Shirley Long, Jean Smith, Jean Marian Smith, Margaret Lovering, Jean Morgan, F. Davies, Jean Martin, Margaret Johnson, Pamela Llanfear.

Six
Worship

St Paul's Church, Commercial Street, about 1860. The road to the right of the church later became Palmyra Place and leads up to Kings Hill. Kings Hill House stands at the top. St Paul's was built in 1836 and is no longer in use.

Portland Street Methodist Free Chapel decorated for Harvest Festival, probably in 1906. The Revd William Vivian is standing between the piers of a model Transporter Bridge. Built in 1853, the chapel was closed for worship in 1950.

Charles Street Baptist Chapel Whitsun Parade before the First World War. The Charles Street Chapel was opened in 1817, and until 1879 all services were held in Welsh. It was closed in 1993, and has recently been acquired by Newport Borough Council.

Stow Hill Baptist Chapel pageant, *Samuel Anointing David*, c. 1928.

Newport Sunday School veterans, 1930s. The Newport Sunday School Union was established in 1833 and held annual Sunday School processions for Sunday School children and their teachers.

Building the Church Hall at Alexandra Road Baptist Church, June 1937. The hall was built by church members headed by 72 year-old Tom Punchard and paid for with £250 raised by the congregation. The Revd David W. Ingram stands to the right.

Charles Street Baptist Chapel decorated for Harvest Festival in the late 1930s.

St Luke's Church, Bridge Street, in the 1950s. St Luke's was built in 1857 and demolished in 1994.

Tabernacle Chapel Whit Monday parade in Dock Street, 22 May 1961. The Tabernacle Chapel stood in this street.

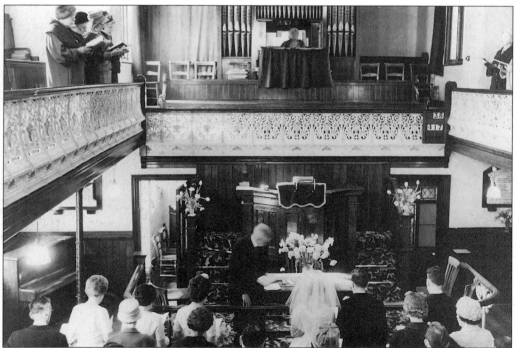

Charles Street Baptist Chapel, photographed during the marriage of Miss Jill Scannell to Mr Brian O'Keefe, 31 March 1962.

Seven
Wartime

Members of the National Reserve marching down Stow Hill, 1914. St Mary's Roman Catholic Church can be seen in the background.

"POST" COMFORTS LEAVING CORDEY'S, JULY 1, 1915.

Boxes of 'comforts' for soldiers abroad leaving the premises of Thomas Cordey, 1 July 1915. Cordey's, the Monmouthshire and South Wales Supply Stores, stocked groceries, teas, coffees, preserved goods, aerated waters, general household requisites and patent medicines. The cart is standing at the back entrance in Cambrian Road, Mr Thomas Cordey stands to the right wearing a boater.

Employees at Lovell's Confectionary Works during the First World War, 1914-18. The black armbands are worn as a sign of bereavement.

Percy Scannell (right) and Reginald Scannell (left), South Wales Borderers, First World War.

82

Taking up tram lines at the junction of George Street and Commercial Road, probably in 1940. When trams had been replaced by a motor bus service in 1937 many of the tram lines were left in place. It seems likely that the picture shows these lines being removed as part of the scrap metal collections during the Second World War. There is an air raid shelter to the left of the photograph.

Left: Nancy Fussell dressed as Britannia to celebrate the end of the First World War, 1918.

The Civic Centre during the Second World War. The curb stones have been painted black and white to give better visibility at night during the blackout.

Air raid wardens unloading civilian gas masks at the Corporation depot in Potter Street, 1939.

Munitions workers at Mannesman's Factory, Commercial Road during the Second World War. As in the First World War, women were required to do the work of men who had joined the armed services.

CORPORATION

Crates of munitions ready to leave Mannesman's Factory, Second World War. Shortages of basic raw materials resulted in a wide variety of boxes being used to transport munitions, including beer crates.

Field of Remembrance at Newport Castle, 1945. One of the women planting a cross is Mrs G. Claude Martyn.

Eight
Shops and Shopping

The Parrot Hotel, Commercial Street, before 1885. The Parrot was famous as a meeting place for Chartist sympathizers in the 1830s and it was here that John Frost was said to have first declared himself a Chartist in 1838. The Town Council also met here occasionally until the Town Hall was built in 1885. The crowd to the right is standing at the entrance to Charles Street. The Body Shop occupies the site today.

Joseph Shewring's shop front at 116 Commercial Street, c. 1888. Joseph Shewring, signwriter, gilder and glass embosser, lived above his shop and stands proudly between his two front doors.

Thomas Gabb's cabinet making business at 115 Commercial Street, completely destroyed by fire in 1889. The remains of Joseph Shewring's shop can be seen to the right.

Evans, shoe retailers, on the corner of
Commercial Street and Emlyn Street, 1891.
William Evans offered both ready-to-wear
and made-to-measure footwear. This was the
first shoe shop in South Wales to offer 'while
you wait' repairs. Note the gas lighting.

NEW PREMISES.
Opened April, 1886.

ESTABLISHED 1869.

G. REYNOLDS,

DRAPER,

149 & 150, COMMERCIAL STREET

Show Rooms for Millinery, Mantles, Ladies'
and Children's Outfitting,

POST ORDERS RECEIVE EVERY ATTENTION.

An advertisement for Reynolds, the drapers
on the corner of Charles Street and
Commercial Street, 1888. Reynolds was a
well known department store in Newport
and employed over a hundred staff at the
time of this advertisement. It was replaced
by Owen Owen in the 1970s, and the T.S.B.
in 1991.

Blotter supplied to customers of Gregory & Roberts, wholesale grocers, 31 Commercial Street, 1884.

The corner of High Street and Thomas Street, before 1903. The wall blocking off the Thomas Street level crossing can be seen on the right hand side. To the left of the photograph stands the old Post Office, built in 1845 and demolished in 1904. On the corner of the two streets is the Great Western Coffee Tavern. The level crossing can be seen on page 53.

The Silver Grill on the corner of
High Street and Station Approach,
1904. The Silver Grill was owned
by Frederick and Octavius Bland
who also owned the Mikado in
High Street. Both establishments
were particularly noted for their
Victoria bride-cake.

Collapsed premises on the corner
of Griffin Street, about 1900.

H. Simmonds in front of his shop at 26 High Street, before the First World War. His father, Alfred Simmonds established the business in 1877. Simmonds supplied Newport Football Club with their playing strip.

High Street, c. 1912. From right to left the buildings are: Newport Electric Theatre; Boodles Teeth Adaptors; Tredegar Arms Hotel; Murrenger House; Joyce & Sons, booksellers; Greenland and Co., stationers; the Greyhound Hotel.

Taylor's Corn Stores at 186 Commercial Road on Coronation Day, 12 May 1937. Alfred Taylor was a well known supplier to poultry keepers and pigeon fanciers. He owned the stores from 1927 until he retired around 1965.

Frederick Hockey, baker and grocer outside his shop in Dolphin Street, probably in the 1930s.

The Market Hall decorated for the Coronation of George VI in 1937.

Nine

Leisure

Charity rugby match at the Newport Infirmary, St Woolos, between merchants and brokers from Dock Street, 21 January 1892. In the second row from the front, fourth from the left, is E.L. Melville Heard, and in the third row, second from the left, is Arthur Wentworth Heard, both sons of William Esau Heard, a well established importer and exporter of goods in Newport. In the back row, fourth from the left, is Arthur Gould, the famous Newport rugby player who was capped for Wales 27 times. Fifth from the left in the back row is Henry Percy Phillips, nicknamed 'the Sparrow' because of his apparent frailty, but who nevertheless won six Welsh rugby caps. Henry Phillips worked for Partridge Jones & Co., colliery proprietors in Newport.

Tredegar Hall and Constitutional Club, Stow Hill, the day it opened, 1890. The hall was originally a concert hall but was turned into a cinema in 1937. In 1958 it became the Majestic Dance Hall.

Programme for a Tredegar Hall concert, 1895.

Dorothy Howells poses in a Newport photographer's studio on a pedal powered motor car, c. 1900. Cars similar to this one were sold for 25/9d, and were advertised as having rubber tyres, steps, a speedometer, and a clock. This model also has a light and a horn.

Pill Harriers baseball team, 1900.

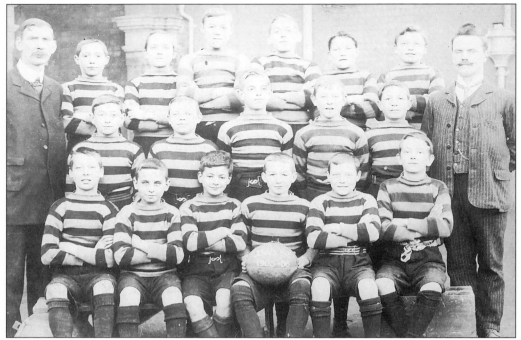

Bolt Street School rugby team, 1905-1906. The Headmaster Mr Morris is standing to the left and the Sports Master Mr Jones to the right. Bolt Street School (now demolished) was affiliated to the Newport Schools Rugby Union along with 17 other Newport schools. Games between schools were played every Saturday morning in Newport parks and finals took place on the Newport Athletic Grounds.

Mr William H. Beer, landlord of the Hare and Greyhound Inn at 37 Commercial Street, standing in a lions cage for a bet in 1907. The lions belonged to the visiting circus of Messrs Bostock and Wombwell.

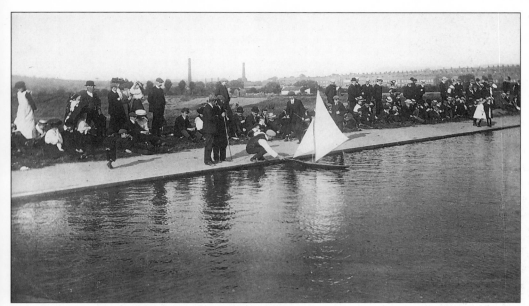

Model boats on the yachting pond at Shaftesbury Park, c. 1910.

SKATING ALTERYN NEWPORT JAN. 11 1908   HUXTABLE BROS.

Skating at Allt-yr-yn on 11 January 1908.

Tredegar Arms, Bassaleg, c. 1910.

Bowling at the Tredegar Arms, c. 1910.

Playing in Herbert Street, c. 1910. Herbert Street was demolished in the 1970s.

Playing in Rogerstone, around 1900. Note the little girl with the hoop and stick in the bottom right hand corner.

Sunday outing on the Monmouthshire Canal, probably near Fourteen Locks, c. 1910.

Monmouthshire Canal, c. 1910.

Posters advertising the Empire and Lyceum in High Street on buildings shortly to be demolished, after 1907. The Corn Exchange and the corner of the new Post Office can be seen to the left.

The South Wales Luncheon Bar and proprietor, George Shaw, Griffin Street, 1912. The bar was demolished in 1935.

The Lyceum Theatre, probably 1920s. The Lyceum was built in 1867, and was originally named the Victoria Hall. It was financed by tramways company director and entrepreneur, Henry Pearce Bolt. It was demolished in 1962. The site is now occupied by the Cannon Cinema.

Publicity photograph of Madova, a singer who appeared at the Empire Theatre in Charles Street, 1920s. The photograph was given to Godfrey Knowles, the hall keeper at the Empire Theatre.

A programme for the Empire Theatre in Charles Street. The Empire eventually closed in 1942 after it was severely damaged by fire.

A publicity photograph of Les Trois Matas given to Godfrey Knowles, the Empire Theatre Hall Keeper, 1920s.

An outing from Potter Street, Pillgwenlly, probably to the West Usk Lighthouse, 1920s.

West Usk Lighthouse, c. 1910. The
lighthouse was built in 1821 and was a
favourite destination for day trips. Today it
is a private house.

High Street in 1923. The Rialto Cinema and part of Lovell's shop were demolished soon after this photograph was taken to improve access to Station Approach. The taxi drivers' cabin can be seen on the right, just inside Station Approach.

Playing 'roll a penny' at a Royal Gwent Hospital fête, probably 1934.

The Mayor, Councillor William Casey congratulating the Carnival Queen, Miss Irene Fairfax, in 1935.

A Dickens Party at the Town Hall, December 1935. The Mayor, Councillor Casey, is greeting Mr Pickwick. The Mayoress stands to the Mayor's left.

Boxing Match, 9 November 1937. The Mayor, Alderman I. Cameron Vincent (seated), with his secretary acting as his second, celebrated the end of his tenure as mayor with three rounds in the ring with Jim Rice, a Newport professional boxer.

Looking towards Bridge Street, 22 April 1962. The Lyceum can be seen on the right, surrounded by scaffolding and ready for demolition. The Queen's Hotel is on the left.

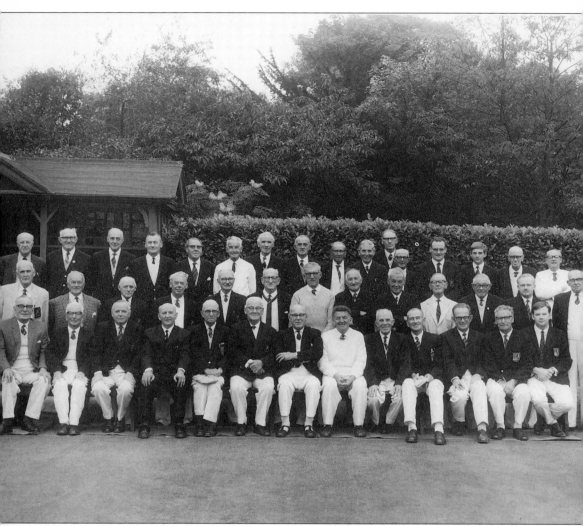

Belle Vue Bowling Club, 1969. From left to right, back row: W. Thomas, R. Parsons, F. Harvey,
C. Greenaway, A. Vernon, C.J. Webb, A. Harris, A.E. Huntbach, R.L. Short, S.J. Hunt, W.
Miles, D.T. Gregory, J. Agland, I. Agland, F. Davies, J. Simons. Middle row: F. Simmonds, W.
Jenkins, F. Dauncey, J. Daniels, C. Noad, C. Jones, A. Skeldon, W. Freeman, W. J. Watkins, C.
Hutchinson, E. Williams, C.G. Harris, J.E. Parkyn. Front row: H.E. Francis, S.J. Porter, L.P.
Thomas, J. Evans, D.T. Trowbridge, E.E. Cashmore, W. Powell, C. Bulley, R. Ray, R.H. Cox, E.
Edge, J. McBain, R.D. Morgan.

Ten
Special Events

Town Council, 2 May 1873. In the centre of the group is a silver 'cradle' presented to Mrs Wyndham Jones by the council to mark the birth of her son during her husband's mayoralty. At this time the council had no official meeting place (the Town Hall was not built until 1885) and this photograph was later superimposed onto a different background so that the group appeared to be in a wood panelled room. The cradle is now in the Museum collections.

Laying the Alice Dry Dock foundation stone, April 1871. The dock was built for the Newport Dry Dock, Wood and Iron Shipbuilding and Ship-repairing Co. The Alice Dry Dock was acquired by Mordey, Carney & Co. in 1884, and stood alongside the Edith and Mary dry docks.

The Alice Dry Dock on the day the foundation stone was laid, April 1871.

'The Largest Bazaar Ever', early 1880s. This fund raising fête was held in the Albert Hall on Commercial Street (now demolished) and proceeds went to the Royal Gwent Hospital and to the Free Library. Mr Thomas Beynon the Mayor, the Duke of Beaufort and Lord Tredegar are sitting on the platform at the far end of the hall.

Bonfire at Twmbarlwm, ignited on 21 June 1887 to celebrate Queen Victoria's Golden Jubilee.

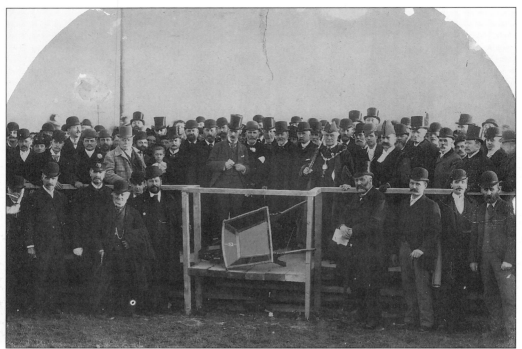

Cutting the first sod, Belle Vue Park, 3 November 1892. The Mayor is Alderman Henry John Davies.

National Eisteddfod at Belle Vue Park, 1897.

114

BOAT SATURDAY. NEWPORT. 19. OCT. 07

PHOTO BALLARD

Lifeboat Saturday, 19 October 1907. A procession, described as a 'demonstration and cycle carnival', left the Cattle Market and paraded along John Street, Bolt Street and Commercial Road, then across Town Bridge and along Caerleon Road as far as Duckpool Road and then back to Commercial Street and the Cattle Market. The fundraising event was organised by the Newport Lifeboat Saturday Fund.

Police parade past the Royal Gwent Hospital, c. 1906. Head Constable Alan Inderwick Sinclair is the mounted officer second from the left.

The last engine to use the railway crossing at the junction of Commercial Street and George Street, 1920s. The Alma Inn, then the William IV, can be seen in the background, bearing an advertisement for Phillips, the Newport brewers. To the left is the showroom of Maybury & Co., Ironmongers, now demolished. Although this railway line was not used commercially after 1907 it seems likely that the photograph was taken when lines and sleepers were being removed from the track in the 1920s.

An ox roast at Shaftesbury Park to celebrate the Coronation of George V in 1911.

Whitewashing a wall in Mellon Street in preparation for Coronation celebrations, 1937.

Residents of Mellon Street during Coronation celebrations in 1937.

Outside the Town Hall during the visit of King George VI to Newport in 1937.

His Majesty King George VI cutting the first sod of the new Civic Centre during his visit to Newport in 1937. The king is using a silver spade supplied by the jewellers Pleasance & Harper. The spade is now in the museum collection.

Newport's Coronation babies, July 1937. The first baby to be born on Coronation day was George Albert Avery, at 12.03 a.m. His mother Mrs P. Avery is standing between the Mayor, Alderman I. Cameron Vincent, and the Mayoress. Mrs Avery was presented with a silver cup and a replica of the anointing spoon used at the Coronation. The seven other mothers are: Mrs Martin, Mrs Isom, Mrs Pinch, Mrs Phillips, Mrs Wilks, Mrs Bowen, Mrs Hancox and Mrs Bonnici. They received £5 each.

Royal Gwent Hospital fête, 7 August 1939, showing Elvira Stephens, aged 9, with the Mayor, Councillor J.R. Wardell, George Dickenson a fête organiser and her mother, Mrs Dorothy Stephens. Elvira had won a talent competition at the fête three years previously and had since become Shirley Temple's understudy.

Eleven
Serving the Community

Newport's first Free Library, Dock Street, 1870. The building was donated to the town by the Athenaeum and Mechanics Institute along with books and furniture. On the right, note the fire brigade escape ladder which was always stored outside the Old Library.

St John's Ambulance Brigade, 1888.

Newport councillors and officials at a site inspection during the building of the Wentwood reservoir, 1896.

Firemen with engines outside the Cattle Market, Pillgwenlly, 1900. The Volunteer Fire Brigade was formed in 1884; previously fire fighting equipment and duties had been under the jurisdiction of the Police. At the time of this photograph there was no fire station. A large bell was fixed above the entrance to the Town Hall police station so that policemen on the beat might warn volunteer firemen in their vicinity of an emergency.

Head Constable Alan Inderwick Sinclair, Mountjoy Place, around 1900. Alan Sinclair was Head Constable of the Police force in Newport from 1875 until 1912.

Installation of reservoir filters in 1910. At this time Newport relied on water from the Wentwood, Pantyrreos and Ynysyfro reservoirs. Until 1910 the water into the town was untreated, and after heavy rain was badly discoloured. The Ynysyfro reservoir was opened by the Newport and Pillgwenlly Waterworks Company in 1848. Among the directors of the company were Samuel Homfray and James Jamieson Cordes.

Water tank reservoir, Stow Hill, May 1911. Water for this tank came from the Ynysyfro reservoir. Before the construction of the reservoir and a system of waterpipes through the town, the population of Newport had to rely on wells and public pumps.

Stow Hill, c. 1910. The roof of the water tank in the previous photograph can be seen behind the trees to the left of St Woolos.

Christmas Day in a ward at the Infirmary on Stow Hill, probably during the First World War. Note the cat sitting on the table in the centre.

Directing the traffic, Ebenezer Terrace, 1930s. The policeman to the right is Constable Harry A. Wall.

Alderman Mrs H.J. Hart, the first woman mayor of Newport, congratulating Mrs Ann Watkins of Courtybella Street, on her 100th birthday, 1938.

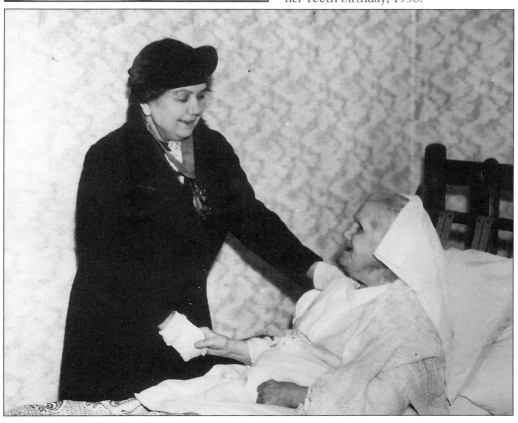

Inspecting a blunderbuss at the Local Government Centenary Exhibition, Newport Museum and Art Gallery, 1935. During the 1870s the blunderbuss used to be fired every night at 10.00 p.m. by the watchman at the Dos Works to let Mr Cordes the owner, who lived at Brynglas, know all was well. The museum assistant is Miss M. Meek.

The Library and Museum and Art Gallery in Dock Street, probably in the early 1960s. This building replaced the library building on page 121. The freehold of the land was presented to the Corporation by Lord Tredegar and the building was opened in November 1882. The premises included a reading room, lending and reference library, committee room and by 1887 a museum. The reading room was supplied with 121 periodicals and was open daily from 9 a.m. until 10 p.m. An average of 292 books were issued daily by the lending library. It seems that the space provided for the museum was inadequate and within five years of its opening the possibility of extending the premises was already being considered. The entire building was demolished in 1968 when the Library, Museum and Art Gallery moved to their present premises in John Frost Square.

Assistants in the old Museum and Art Gallery in Dock Street, 1950s. Miss M. Meek stands in the centre.

Acknowledgements

I would like to thank the following individuals and organisations for their help in the compilation of this book, and for permission to reproduce photographs:

Louise Baggs, Glyn Bennett, Mike Bowers, Mrs P. Channing, Carol Hiles, Rodney Hudson, Les James, Joan Lougher, Maureen McManus, the family of the late Henry Morrish, Newport Reference Library, Wendy Lewis, Jill O'Keefe, Colin Lloyd, Rachel Silverson, Gareth Solway, Robert Trett, Annette Wells, Stanley Wright.

Stock List

(Titles are listed according to the pre-1974 county boundaries)

BERKSHIRE

Wantage
Irene Hancock
ISBN 0-7524-0146 7

CARDIGANSHIRE

Aberaeron and Mid Ceredigion
William Howells
ISBN 0-7524-0106-8

CHESHIRE

Ashton-under-Lyne and Mossley
Alice Lock
ISBN 0-7524-0164-5

Around Bebington
Pat O'Brien
ISBN 0-7524-0121-1

Crewe
Brian Edge
ISBN 0-7524-0052-5

Frodsham and Helsby
Frodsham and District Local History Group
ISBN 0-7524-0161-0

Macclesfield Silk
Moira Stevenson and Louanne Collins
ISBN 0-7524-0315 X

Marple
Steve Cliffe
ISBN 0-7524-0316-8

Runcorn
Bert Starkey
ISBN 0-7524-0025-8

Warrington
Janice Hayes
ISBN 0-7524-0040-1

West Kirby to Hoylake
Jim O'Neil
ISBN 0-7524-0024-X

Widnes
Anne Hall and the Widnes Historical Society
ISBN 0-7524-0117-3

CORNWALL

Padstow
Malcolm McCarthy
ISBN 0-7524-0033-9

St Ives Bay
Jonathan Holmes
ISBN 0-7524-0186-6

COUNTY DURHAM

Bishop Auckland
John Land
ISBN 0-7524-0312-5

Around Shildon
Vera Chapman
ISBN 0-7524-0115-7

CUMBERLAND

Carlisle
Dennis Perriam
ISBN 0-7524-0166-1

DERBYSHIRE

Around Alfreton
Alfreton and District Heritage Trust
ISBN 0-7524-0041-X

Barlborough, Clowne, Creswell and Whitwell
Les Yaw
ISBN 0-7524-0031-2

Around Bolsover
Bernard Haigh
ISBN 0-7524-0021-5

Around Derby
Alan Champion and Mark Edworthy
ISBN 0-7524-0020-7

Long Eaton
John Barker
ISBN 0-7524-0110-6

Ripley and Codnor
David Buxton
ISBN 0-7524-0042-8

Shirebrook
Geoff Sadler
ISBN 0-7524-0028-2

Shirebrook: A Second Selection
Geoff Sadler
ISBN 0-7524-0317-6

Winchester from the Sollars Collection
John Brimfield
ISBN 0-7524-0173-4

HEREFORDSHIRE

Ross-on-Wye
Tom Rigby and Alan Sutton
ISBN 0-7524-0002-9

HERTFORDSHIRE

Buntingford
Philip Plumb
ISBN 0-7524-0170-X

Hampstead Garden Suburb
Mervyn Miller
ISBN 0-7524-0319-2

Hemel Hempstead
Eve Davis
ISBN 0-7524-0167-X

Letchworth
Mervyn Miller
ISBN 0-7524-0318-4

Welwyn Garden City
Angela Eserin
ISBN 0-7524-0133-5

KENT

Hythe
Joy Melville and Angela Lewis-Johnson
ISBN 0-7524-0169-6

North Thanet Coast
Alan Kay
ISBN 0-7524-0112-2

Shorts Aircraft
Mike Hooks
ISBN 0-7524-0193-9

LANCASHIRE

Lancaster and the Lune Valley
Robert Alston
ISBN 0-7524-0015-0

Morecambe Bay
Robert Alston
ISBN 0-7524-0163-7

Manchester
Peter Stewart
ISBN 0-7524-0103-3

LINCOLNSHIRE

Louth
David Cuppleditch
ISBN 0-7524-0172-6

Stamford
David Gerard
ISBN 0-7524-0309-5

LONDON
(Greater London and Middlesex)

Battersea and Clapham
Patrick Loobey
ISBN 0-7524-0010-X

Canning Town
Howard Bloch and Nick Harris
ISBN 0-7524-0057-6

Chiswick
Carolyn and Peter Hammond
ISBN 0-7524-0001-0

Forest Gate
Nick Harris and Dorcas Sanders
ISBN 0-7524-0049-5

Greenwich
Barbara Ludlow
ISBN 0-7524-0045-2

Highgate and Muswell Hill
Joan Schwitzer and Ken Gay
ISBN 0-7524-0119-X

Islington
Gavin Smith
ISBN 0-7524-0140-8

Lewisham
John Coulter and Barry Olley
ISBN 0-7524-0059-2

Leyton and Leytonstone
Keith Romig and Peter Lawrence
ISBN 0-7524-0158-0

Newham Dockland
Howard Bloch
ISBN 0-7524-0107-6

Norwood
Nicholas Reed
ISBN 0-7524-0147-5

Peckham and Nunhead
John D. Beasley
ISBN 0-7524-0122-X

Piccadilly Circus
David Oxford
ISBN 0-7524-0196-3

Stoke Newington
Gavin Smith
ISBN 0-7524-0159-9

Sydenham and Forest Hill
John Coulter and John Seaman
ISBN 0-7524-0036-3

Wandsworth
Patrick Loobey
ISBN 0-7524-0026-6

Wanstead and Woodford
Ian Dowling and Nick Harris
ISBN 0-7524-0113-0

MONMOUTHSHIRE

Vanished Abergavenny
Frank Olding
ISBN 0-7524-0034-7

Abertillery, Aberbeeg and Llanhilleth
Abertillery and District Museum Society and Simon Eckley
ISBN 0-7524-0134-3

Blaina, Nantyglo and Brynmawr
Trevor Rowson
ISBN 0-7524-0136-X

NORFOLK

North Norfolk
Cliff Richard Temple
ISBN 0-7524-0149-1

NOTTINGHAMSHIRE

Nottingham 1897–1947
Douglas Whitworth
ISBN 0-7524-0157-2

OXFORDSHIRE

Banbury
Tom Rigby
ISBN 0-7524-0013-4

PEMBROKESHIRE

Saundersfoot and Tenby
Ken Daniels
ISBN 0-7524-0192-0

RADNORSHIRE

Llandrindod Wells
Chris Wilson
ISBN 0-7524-0191-2

SHROPSHIRE

Leominster
Eric Turton
ISBN 0-7524-0307-9

Ludlow
David Lloyd
ISBN 0-7524-0155-6

Oswestry
Bernard Mitchell
ISBN 0-7524-0032-0

North Telford: Wellington, Oakengates, and Surrounding Areas
John Powell and Michael A. Vanns
ISBN 0-7524-0124-6

South Telford: Ironbridge Gorge, Madeley, and Dawley
John Powell and Michael A. Vanns
ISBN 0-7524-0125-4

SOMERSET

Bath
Paul De'Ath
ISBN 0-7524-0127-0

Around Yeovil
Robin Ansell and Marion Barnes
ISBN 0-7524-0178-5

STAFFORDSHIRE

Cannock Chase
Sherry Belcher and Mary Mills
ISBN 0-7524-0051-7

Around Cheadle
George Short
ISBN 0-7524-0022-3

The Potteries
Ian Lawley
ISBN 0-7524-0046-0

East Staffordshire
Geoffrey Sowerby and Richard Farman
ISBN 0-7524-0197-1

SUFFOLK

Lowestoft to Southwold
Humphrey Phelps
ISBN 0-7524-0108-4

Walberswick to Felixstowe
Humphrey Phelps
ISBN 0-7524-0109-2

SURREY

Around Camberley
Ken Clarke
ISBN 0-7524-0148-3

Around Cranleigh
Michael Miller
ISBN 0-7524-0143-2

Epsom and Ewell
Richard Essen
ISBN 0-7524-0111-4

Farnham by the Wey
Jean Parratt
ISBN 0-7524-0185-8

Industrious Surrey: Historic Images of the County at Work
Chris Shepheard
ISBN 0-7524-0009-6

Reigate and Redhill
Mary G. Goss
ISBN 0-7524-0179-3

Richmond and Kew
Richard Essen
ISBN 0-7524-0145-9

SUSSEX

Billingshurst
Wendy Lines
ISBN 0-7524-0301-X

WARWICKSHIRE

Central Birmingham 1870–1920
Keith Turner
ISBN 0-7524-0053-3

Old Harborne
Roy Clarke
ISBN 0-7524-0054-1

WILTSHIRE

Malmesbury
Dorothy Barnes
ISBN 0-7524-0177-7

Great Western Swindon
Tim Bryan
ISBN 0-7524-0153-X

Midland and South Western Junction Railway
Mike Barnsley and Brian Bridgeman
ISBN 0-7524-0016-9

WORCESTERSHIRE

Around Malvern
Keith Smith
ISBN 0-7524-0029-0

YORKSHIRE
(EAST RIDING)

Hornsea
G.L. Southwell
ISBN 0-7524-0120-3

YORKSHIRE
(NORTH RIDING)

Northallerton
Vera Chapman
ISBN 0-7524-055-X

Scarborough in the 1970s and 1980s
Richard Percy
ISBN 0-7524-0325-7

YORKSHIRE
(WEST RIDING)

Barnsley
Barnsley Archive Service
ISBN 0-7524-0188-2

Bingley
Bingley and District Local History Society
ISBN 0-7524-0311-7

Bradford
Gary Firth
ISBN 0-7524-0313-3

Castleford
Wakefield Metropolitan District Council
ISBN 0-7524-0047-9

Doncaster
Peter Tuffrey
ISBN 0-7524-0162-9

Harrogate
Malcolm Neesam
ISBN 0-7524-0154-8

Holme Valley
Peter and Iris Bullock
ISBN 0-7524-0139-4

Horsforth
Alan Cockroft and Matthew Young
ISBN 0-7524-0130-0

Knaresborough
Arnold Kellett
ISBN 0-7524-0131-9

Around Leeds
Matthew Young and Dorothy Payne
ISBN 0-7524-0168-8

Penistone
Matthew Young and David Hambleton
ISBN 0-7524-0138-6

**Selby from the William Rawling
Collection**
Matthew Young
ISBN 0-7524-0198-X

Central Sheffield
Martin Olive
ISBN 0-7524-0011-8

Around Stocksbridge
Stocksbridge and District History Society
ISBN 0-7524-0165-3

TRANSPORT

Filton and the Flying Machine
Malcolm Hall
ISBN 0-7524-0171-8

Gloster Aircraft Company
Derek James
ISBN 0-7524-0038-X

Great Western Swindon
Tim Bryan
ISBN 0-7524-0153-X

Midland and South Western Junction Railway
Mike Barnsley and Brian Bridgeman
ISBN 0-7524-0016-9

Shorts Aircraft
Mike Hooks
ISBN 0-7524-0193-9

This stock list shows all titles available in the United Kingdom as at 30 September 1995.

ORDER FORM

The books in this stock list are available from your local bookshop. Alternatively they are available by mail order at a totally inclusive price of £10.00 per copy.

For overseas orders please add the following postage supplement for each copy ordered:
> European Union £0.36 (this includes the Republic of Ireland)
> Royal Mail Zone 1 (for example, U.S.A. and Canada) £1.96
> Royal Mail Zone 2 (for example, Australia and New Zealand) £2.47

Please note that all of these supplements are actual Royal Mail charges with no profit element to the Chalford Publishing Company. Furthermore, as the Air Mail Printed Papers rate applies, we are restricted from enclosing any personal correspondence other than to indicate the senders name.

Payment can be made by cheque, Visa or Mastercard. Please indicate your method of payment on this order form.

If you are not entirely happy with your purchase you may return it within 30 days of receipt for a full refund.

Please send your order to:

> The Chalford Publishing Company,
> St Mary's Mill,
> Chalford,
> Stroud,
> Gloucestershire
> GL6 8NX

This order form should perforate away from the book. However, if you are reluctant to damage the book in any way we are quite happy to accept a photocopy order form or a letter containing the necessary information.

PLEASE WRITE CLEARLY USING BLOCK CAPITALS

Name and address of the person ordering the books listed below:

_____

_____

_____ Post code _____

Please also supply your telephone number in case we have difficulty fully understanding your requirements.   Tel.: _____ - _____

Name and address of where the books are to be despatched to (if different from above):

_____

_____

_____ Post code _____

Please indicate here if you would like to receive future information on books published by the Chalford Publishing Company.

____ Yes, please put me on your mailing list   ____ No, please just send the books ordered below

Title	ISBN	Quantity
....	0-7524-_____-___	_____
....	0-7524-_____-___	_____
....	0-7524-_____-___	_____
....	0-7524-_____-___	_____
....	0-7524-_____-___	_____
	Total number of books	_____

Cost of books delivered in UK = Number of books ordered @ £10 each =£ _____

Overseas postage supplement (if relevant)   =£ _____

TOTAL PAYMENT   =£ _____

Method of Payment   ❏ Cheque   ❏ Visa   ❏ Mastercard   **VISA**

Please make cheques payable to *The Chalford Publishing Company*   MasterCard

Name of Card Holder   _____

Card Number ❏❏❏❏❏❏❏❏❏❏❏❏❏❏❏❏❏❏❏

Expiry date ❏❏ / ❏❏

I authorise payment of £_____ from the above card

Signed _____